Amenities & Projects

Of

Social Welfare Department

In

Pakistan

Afshan Qureshi

Scholar of Sociology

Bahauddin Zakaria University

Multan

"Until The Great Mass of People shall be filled with the Sense of Responsibility for each other Welfare, Social Justice can never be attained"

Helen Killer

DEDICATED

TO

MY

SWEET

&

LOVING

MAMA

ACKNOWLEDGEMENT

I am very gratified to Almighty Allah, the most merciful and beneficial for giving me ability and courage to complete this work for writing a book.

I am very thankful to my Mother who helps me in every step of my life.

I am also thankful to the Community Development Department; who give me a chance for observing different facilities and projects of Social Welfare Department.

Afshan Qureshi

PREFACE

Community Development Department gave me an opportunity to observe different amenities and projects of Social Welfare Department. After observation, I felt that there are some basic problems and our strategies are not right which we are applying for the welfare of people. I think about these problems that how we can work out on these problems.

CONTENTS

INTRODUCTION

Dco (District Coordinator Officer)

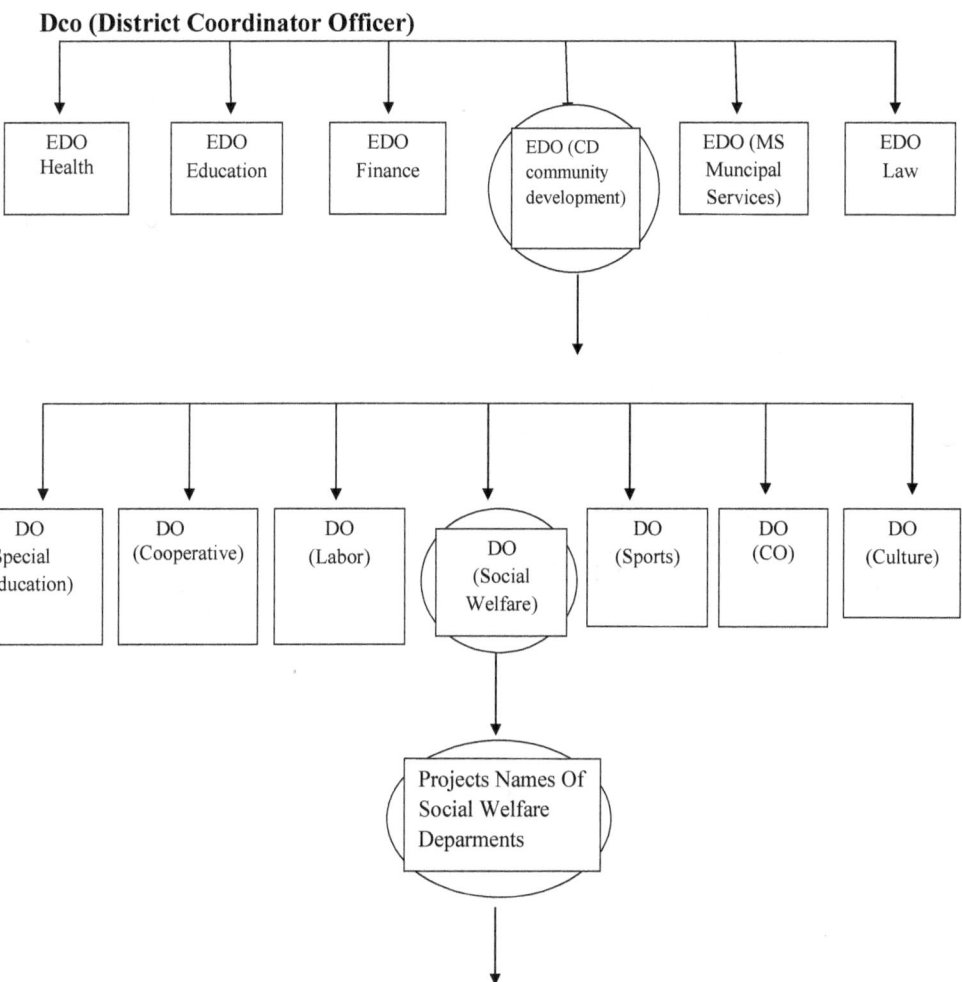

S. No	Institutions Names
1.	District Office, Social Welfare, Women Development & Bait-ul-Mal Multan
2.	Industrial Home for Vocational Skill Development (Sanatzar)
3.	Convalescent Home Multan/ Drug Rehabilitation Centre

7

4.	Dara -ul-Aman
5.	Dara -ul-Falah
6.	Dara -ul-Panah
7.	Day Care Centre (Ghuncha)
8.	Nigheban
9.	Aafiuat
10.	Hostel for Working Women
11.	Women Jail

12.	Community Development Program
	    a) Local Government
	    b) UCD 1
	    c) UCD 2
	    d) Rural Community Development Project Chak 5 Fiaz
	    e) Community Development Project Shujabad

13.	Citizens Community Boards (CCBs)

14.	Medical Social Welfare Projects
	    a) Nishter Hospital Multan
	    b) Minar, Nishter Hospital Multan
	    c) Multan Institute of Cardiology
	    d) Civil Hospital
	    e) Tehsil Head Quarter Shujabad

15.	Vocational Centre From TMA
16.	Gehwara
17.	District Rescue Centre for women in Local Government Multan
18.	Crisis Centre for Women in District MDA

INDUSTRIAL HOME (SANATZAR MULTAN)

INTRODUCTION

Economic prosperity is directly related to social development. Without participation of all hands , both men and women , Pakistan can't be go into developed countries. we have long been thinking of exploring the possibilities for bringing women into the main stream of economic development activities by enabling them to acquire skills and vacations by which they could be a considerable man power resource of country. The social welfare department Punjab has been enter to achieve the aim through openings Sanatzars/Socio-Economic Centers since 1979.

OBJECTIVES

1. The scheme of Sanatzar has been designed to afford a focal point of socio-economic up-lift of women in district.
2. Opening of similar sub-centers at Town and Tehsil level with the cooperation of V.S.W.A/NGOs.
3. Providing order-work on wages to trained women in the manufacture of products for sale in the market.
4. Providing training to women in local and specialized crafts.
5. Organizing/ participating melas/Fairs/Exhibitions of products at the local, District and province level.
6. Preparing of standard design of local crafts and supply of their samples to market to obtain bulk orders.
7. Coordination with Government and connected organizations in boosting market ability of products.

OFFICE ORGANIZATION

S.No	Post	BPS	Strength	Remarks
1	Manager	18	1	Filled
2	Designer	17	1-v	Vacant since several years
3	Marketing organizer	11	1-v	Dual

4	Assistant/Accountant	14	1	Filled
5	Craft supervisor	11	1-v	Filled
6	Tailor Cum Cutter	11	1	Filled
7	Store keeper	07	1	Filled
8	Junior clerk	07	1	Filled
9	Driver	06	1	Filled
10	Naib Qasid	02	2	Filled
11	Sweeper	02	1	Filled
12	Chowkidar	02	1	Filled
	TOTAL:-		16	15

SERVICES ON SELF HELP BASIS

Sr.#	SERVICES	THROUGH
1	Beautician	Through 2 contract teachers
2	Computer	Through a female computer operator of DRC.
3	Cooking	Through Contract Teachers.
4	Reta work	Through Contract Teachers.
5	Tila Silma	Through Contract Teachers.
6	Local Craft	Through Contract Teachers.
7	Dress Designing	Through Contract Teachers.
8	Spoken English	Through Contract Teachers.
9	Display center	Through Contract Sales Man.
10	Cutting Tailoring	----Do----

SERVICES AND CHARGES

S.NO	SERVICES	FEE PER MONTH
1	Admission	100/-
2	Cutting Sewing/Gen: Tailoring	200/-
3	Gents Tailoring	200/-

4	Dismatic	300/-
5	Special Training	200/-
6	Dress Designing	400/-
7	Reta Work	500/-
8	Tila Silma / Ada Work	500/-
9	Beautician	1000/-
10	Local craft/Fine Arts	500/-
11	Cooking	500/-
12	Computer	500/-
13	Spoken English	600/-
14	Certificate	100/-

Note: 20% Admission of deserving trainees are free.

Present Admission: 237

Sr. No.	Institution	Unit	Beneficiaries
1	Sanatzar	1	636
2	Sub-sanatzar	9	741
	TOTAL	10	1377

OTHER ACTIVITES CURRENT YEAR

1. Organized competitions Punjab youth Festivals,2012 very successfully.
2. Celebrate Eid-Milad, Women day, Anti Dengue seminars.
3. Distribution of Certificates.
4. Monthly meeting of advisory committee.
5. Participated most successfully regarding stalls in the exhibition at Lahore.
6. Organized/Arranged Civil Defense Training for Trainees of Sanatzar.
7. Arranged 2 visits of Executive members of Women chamber of congress Multan.
8. Inauguration of library, spoken English and deskmatic classes.

9. Satisfactory visits of Begum D.C.O.

ISSUES

1. Lack of pick and drop service for the trainees.
2. Non A.C computer lab.
3. Non availability of furniture and fixture of meeting hall.
4. Non appointment of designer (BPS.17).
5. Temporary duty of Marketing Organizer at Khanewal.
6. Non availability budget of transfer T.A/Grant and repair of vehicle.

SUGGESTIONS:

Cosmetics & Beauty Products have many harmful ingredients & we think that these things are helpful for looking beautiful but in reality it is the harmful for our skin. There are over 150 ingredients in every product. According to experts, many of these are toxics & potentially damaging to our health. These are included on artificially fragrances, coloring, pesticides, preservatives & other synthetic chemicals. According to a research, every woman absorb at least 2 kilogram of chemicals through toiletries & cosmetics every year & women became the victim, of many diseases such as; blindness, different types of cancer such as mouth cancer, brain cancer, lungs cancer, ovarian cancer, breast cancer etc, harmful for lungs, liver, nausea, asthma, mood swings, headache, neurological damage, carcinogenic, coughing, hepatitis, different types of allergies, skin allergies, rashes etc.

So, Government should banned the beautiation course from Sanatzar & from every institutes & also those shops who sell these products because this type of course is not a skill which give the help to females for earning but it gives invitations of many diseases for both customer & beautiationist. For this, there is need to aware the people about its harm, damage or loss. From this action we will save from "Many Diseases" & "Eradicate of Poverty" because mostly part of our income is wasted for purchasing these harmful things & after this we loose on the other part of income on the diseases which we get after using these harmful things & then we become the victim of poverty. From this action, the ratio of poverty & diseases would be decreased & mostly people of our society would be healthy.

HEALTH WELFARE COMMITIES

To provide medicine/ treatment facilities for deserving patients, health welfare committees in the following hospitals have been established which are being funded by Zakat Department, District Bait-ul-mal Committee & Pakistan Bait-ul-mal.

- Nishter Hospital Multan
- MINAR, Nishter Hospital Multan
- Multan Institute of Cardiology
- THQ Hospital Shujabad

NISHTER HOSPITAL MULTAN

INTRODUCTION

The construction of the Nishtar Hospital block started in 1953. The basic idea and it's plan was provided by Dr. M. J. Bhutta. He had already collected many ideas during his tour of U.K. by visiting many hospitals there. Mr. Inamullah, Mr. Jamaal-ud-Din and Mr. Murat Khan also participated in the construction. On the 1st of October, 1953, Nishtar Hospital started functioning with 80 beds. In 1954, Medicine, Surgery, Gynecology, Tuberculosis, Pediatrics, Ophthalmology, ENT, Anesthesia and Radiology departments also started functioning. With the construction of the hospital building, many other buildings including the boy hostels, administration block, and kitchen block. Now, Nishtar Hospital Building is three story building. The Nishter Hospital holds a total capacity of 1103 beds, however extra beds have been added in each department due to a high public demand, and the hospital now has more than 1800 beds. There are 29 wards plus an Out Patients Department. There are 15 Operation Theatres.

Our Focus on Social Welfare in Nishter Hospital Multan

In Nishter Hospital Multan, there is focus on the 3 projects which works on the welfare of patients.

- Medical Social Services Project
- Division of Blood Transfusion Unit
- Model Drug Abuse Center

Medical Social Services Project

- Administrative Department
- Provide medical Facilities & medicines to non-affordable patients
- 3 resources for helping Patients
  1- Zakat Fund
  2- Bait-ul-mal Fund
      i. Pakistan Bait-ul-mal (those treatments which are very costly for example; Hepatitis etc. or have need of 4 to 5 lacks for getting treatment & patients canno tafford this treatment then this department make the report & send to Pakistan Bait-ul-mal)
      ii. Pnnjab Bait-ul-mal
      iii. District Bait-ul-mal (they provide patients 10 to 20 thousand for getting treatment)
  3- Patient Welfare Society
      - Contact form classes
      - Collect Donations
- In door patients (give them 3 thousands rupees for help that they purchase medicines easily. If they have need more than 3 thousand eg. 10 thousand then help at the recommendation of doctor)
- Outdoor patients (provide them weekly 2 thousand for treatment if they need more for treatment eg. 10 to 20 thousand then help them at the recommendation of doctor through zakat fund)
- Provide the free medicines of 15 thousands to cancer patients.
- 10 thousands give the kidney patients for doing treatment.
- Counseling (provide the guidance to poor patients who don't know what they have to do, where they have need to go)

BUDGET: 1 Crore (after every 6 month they get 50 million)

Division of Blood Transfusion Unit

The medical social welfare officer of blood transfusion unit assists the hospitals in enlisting genuine blood donors. This project provides blood free of charge to deserving patients. Medical social welfare officer starts campaigns in different collages that donors give the blood. They also exchange the blood with other family members. Call the family members & which person's blood group match with patient, give them.

Model Drug Abuse Center

The menace of drug addiction is touching new heights in wake of alarming figure of addicts leading to miserable life. One Model Drug Abuse Center has been set up in Nishter Hospital Multan in order to provide diagnostic treatment & rehabilitated services to the drug addicts in cooperation with psychiatrists.

There are some objectives of this department.

- Addicts who want to get treatment
- Provide them free medicines
- Case histories
- Motivate lectures to provide patients & also his/her family against drugs

MINAR HOSPITAL MULTAN

INTRODUCTION

MINAR (Multan Institute of Nuclear and Radiotherapy) Hospital Multan is located in Nishter Hospital Multan. It works under Federal Government Commission Pakistan. It deals with the patients of cancer, diagnose the disease & after this provide them treatment. Those patients who are poor & cannot afford the treatment then try to provide them free treatment.

CARDIOLOGY HOSPITAL MULTAN

Cardiology Hospitals in Pakistan:

In Pakistan, there are 4 cardiac centers.

- In Karachi

- In Rawalpindi
- In Lahore
- In Multan

➢ One hospital is under construction in Peshawar.

Cardiology Hospital Multan

Chaudhry Pervaiz Elahi was founder of the project of Multan Institute of Cardiology. This project was established in 2006. Multan Institute of Cardiology is valuable gift for the people of Southern Punjab, which will go a long way in improving health care facilities, particularly in treatment of cardiovascular diseases. The availability of modern diagnostic & therapeutic modulation along with personalized patients care would help to serve the masses of not only Southern Punjab but also for other areas in Baluchistan, Sindh, Pakhtoon Khwa (NWFP). The institute will go take measure to spread awareness regarding prevention of heart diseases.

Multan Institute of Cardiology have

- 201 beds
- Angiography Machine
- EET
- ECHO
- X-Ray
- Dental Unit
- ECG
- Laboratory
- Pharmacy

Mission Statement

To provide the benefit of latest research and best health care services in the field of cardio-vascular medicine to the people of South Punjab and all areas of Sindh , Baluchistan and NWFP.

Aims

- To provide medical facilities of cardiac care to people of South Punjab and all area of other provinces.
- Post graduate education and training of medical , surgical , nursing and para-medical staff.
- To provide facilities of research in the field of cardiology.

Social Welfare Department of Cardiology Hospital Multan

Social welfare department should have the skills to be professional and the feelings of humanity. They have to work for the well being of people and try to solve their problems which are related to their health or for their social welfare.

Aims/Objectives

- To prepare care histories of patients having financial , psychological and social needs in accordance with case work techniques plan and organize , social services keeping in view individual needs as well as giving them social therapy.
- To organize patient welfare society in hospital and help the members in its functioning and fund raising campaigns.
- To visit of the words with hospital staff and after indicating deserving patients provide them assistance according to their individual needs.
- To set up the information / guidance desk at the cardiac out door for assistance of patient visiting hospital for their treatment.
- To provide ever required assistance to the needy patients particularly arrangements and free investigations pathology tests/x.ray/Ultrasound/CT/ETT/ECG/Emergency and scans etc.
- To dispose of dead bodies unclaimed.
- To help the patients in admission and proportions of estimated cost report of treatment through Bait-ul-mal.
- Co-ordination with voluntary social welfare agencies, hospital administration and district administration.

- To make categories of cardiac patients accordingly and provide them free medicine and treatment as well as to recommend the application of Zakat and Bait-ul-mal patients for Lahore.
- Economic categorization in patients after this their treatment is continued in free.
- Some patients have to pay 30% for test.

Budget of Cardiology Hospital Multan

➤ 50 Lacks but not in utilization.

Daily Average Patients

➤ 300

SUGGESTIONS:

- Every hospital need 2 medical social welfare officers, one male and one female, that male person deals with males and female deal with females, but NISHTER,MINAR,CARDIOLOGY and CIVIL HOSPITAL have just one medical social welfare officer. So, that's why there should be at least 2 social welfare officers in every hospital.
- Heart patients have need of silence but the thing which I observed that in hospital there was lots of noise of people because lots of people come along with patients in hospital and many people start fighting with each other, for this there should be a department at gate which check that how many people are with patients and this department give permission for only one or 2 people to be with patient in hospital & said to other people that they go home & also said them that they have no permission to stay here. So, through this action, we can bring some kind of silence or peace in hospital or every work should be done in a disciplined manner.

DEPARTMENT OF PUNJAB BAIT-UL-MAL

Social Welfare is the process of Social Development through which the potential of the people is stimulated to promote effective participation in the process of social change and improvement of quality of life. The concept of Social Welfare in Pakistan is drawn from the cardinal principles of Islam based on Adl-o-Ehsan and Haqooq-ul-Ibad, making the state and society together responsible for the welfare of the people.The Constitution of Pakistan also enjoins on the state to alleviate the sufferings of all citizens irrespective of gender, caste, creed or race. There are 3 departments of Social Welfare, Women Development & Bait-ul-Maal. Now, women development department is become the new ministry & this department is not under the social welfare department. But, in this chapter our focus is on Punjab Bait-ul-mal Dapartment.

OBJECTIVES

There are some objectives of Punjab Bait-ul-mal Dapartment.

- Poverty eradication.
- To make the better condition of poor people.
- Relief & rehabilitation of the poor, widows & orphans.
- Educational assistance to the poor & deserving students.
- Charitable Purpose.
- For any other purpose of public utility particularly for disadvantages section of the society.

RATE OF STIPEND WHICH PROVIDE TO POOR PEOPLE

The rates of stipend which provide to poor people are as followed.

- For disabled people → at least 3 thousand or more then 5 thousand
- For widows that for learning skills or starting any project & unemployed people → at least 20 thousand
- For marriages of daughters → at least 5 thousand
- For poor patients → at least 10 thousand or more then 20 thousand if he/she is in critical condition (from the 8% fund of patients, 3% fund is for that women who became the victim of violence e.g. acid throwing etc)
- For NGOs → at least 50 thousand

- For students
  - 6th to 8th class → 100 rupees per month
  - Matric → 150 rupees per month
  - F.A, F. Sc, ICS → 1000 rupees per month for those who live in hostels & 500 rupees for those who cannot live in hostels
  - For University students → 1200 rupees per month for those who live in hostels & 600 rupees for those who cannot live in hostels
  - For those students who are taking training in Vocational Education/ Training Centers → 800 rupees per month for those who live in hostels & 500 rupees for those who cannot live in hostels.

BUDGET: 35 Lacks

SUGGESTIONS

Punjab Bait-ul-mal Department which provide money to poor people, it is not enough for fulfilling of their necessaries. To distribute this low stipend between poor people is not the solution of eradicate poverty. From this method, the basic necessities of people cannot be fulfilled & the concept of beggary is created. According to my point of view, if start any project of the income of the budget of bait-ul-mal & give the work to needy or deserving people. From this project, the concept of beggary would be finished, unemployment should be control. The concept of self-esteem would also increase between people & people feel happiness that they are earning with their own hands, their life style would be better & poverty would be control very much. Which profit they would get from this department, should provide the help in the treatment of poor patients & also studies in students.

HOSTEL FOR WORKING WOMEN

The Women Development Department has established hostels for working women in the Province to provide residential facilities to working women who are posted or doing jobs away from their home towns and do not have accommodation at their stations of posting. Due to the non-availability of well protected and safe living place, working women normally do not take jobs away from their home towns. To provide facilities of suitable and secure accommodation on subsidized and affordable charges to working women, these hostels have been established in the following cities of the Province.

- Multan
- Bahawalpur
- Gujranwala
- Faisalabad
- Lahore
- Rawalpindi

HOSTEL FOR WORKING WOMEN IN MULTAN

Hostel for working women in Multan was established in 1975. Firstly, it was the part of Social Welfare Department, now it would become the part of Women Development Department. It has total 24 rooms. The charges of rooms are divided in 3 categories.

1. If 3 women share the room, then they all females have to pay 500 rupees per month.
2. If 2 women share the room, then they all females have to pay 800 rupees per month.
3. If just 1 woman live in one room then she have to pay 1000 rupees per month.

The quota for working women to stay in the hostel

- If women are working the job in government sector then they can stay for 3 years.
- If women are working the job in private sector then they can stay for 1 year.
    - If they want they can increase their period of staying.

BUDGET: 20 lack & 32 thousand

STAFF

- 1 Clark
- 1 Sweeper
- 1 Cook

ISSUES & SUGGESTIONS

- There should be more rooms in hostels.
- There should be a security guard.
- There should be improving the system of the drainage of water.
- There should provide the health facilities.

DAY CARE CENTRE (GHUNCHA)

Those women who are employment somewhere on whole or part time basis consider proper look after of the children a great problem. None is available at home to take care of their babies in their absence. This institute has been established at Multan in 1979, to provide motherly treatment to their children. The Day Care Center has been housed in the building of Hostel for Working Women, M.D.A Road Multan.

STAFF

- 1 Supervisor
- 1 Clark
- 1 guardian
- 1 security guard

BUDGET: 14 lack & 89 thousand

ISSUES & SUGGESTIONS

- There should be health care facilities for children.

CENTER FOR WOMEN IN DISTRESS (DARA-UL-PANAH)

The aim of the establishment of this project is to protect women against violence & to provide free legal aid, free health care facilities & resistance to resolve the social problems being faced by women in distress.

OBJECTIVES OF THIS PROJECT:

1. To register the complains of women & send them in any institution for their help according to their complains.
2. To provide free legal help.
3. To provide free medical help.
4. To provide free help of getting vocational trainings.
5. To provide help in getting admission of the children of the female who are in troubles.
6. To provide guidance that how to solve their problems from government institutes.
7. To provide help in getting economical aid through Bait-ul-mal department.
8. Try to get economical aid to them for making their bright future through their home business about vocational works.
9. To provide free computer trainings to poor girls.
10. To provide the adult education & libraries for women.

TYPES OF CASES:

Types of cases which handled by Dara-ul-Panah are as followed.

- Domestic Cases
- Counseling Cases
- Rape Cases
- Legal Cases such as security cases.

SUGGESTIONS:

- According to my point of view, it is not enough that this department should provide the help to females who became the victim of violence. We have to need to finish the root of violence. For finishing the concept of violence, we have to need to play with the mind of people. In our society, mostly people are listened every advice of molvi hazrat & ulmas & act upon them. So, we should have to take as like people who have fully knowledge about this topic, violence & religion & should change his get up like molvis & then he should go in villages & cities, call the ulma & molvies of this village or city & gather the people at one place. In front of people, ask them questions & then you give the right information to people in the conversation style & try to prove them wrong because these people use the religion just for their benefit. I hope people will listen him & try to act upon it.

- The subject of gender studies would be a compulsory subject in school & collages.
- Our media should show as like programs which promote the equality between male & female & try to finish the roots of violence.

SOCIAL SERVICES CENTERS FOR LOST & KIDNAPPED CHILDREN

(NIGHEHBAN)

INTRODUCTION:

To provide socio services for lost, escaped & kidnapped children. This center has been established at Kutchari Road Near Health Department Multan, where diet, accommodation, recreational facilities are being providing to such children & they are rehabilitated by handing over them to their parents & guardians.

STAFF:

- 1 Social Welfare Officer
- 2 Supervisor (1 Male or 1 Female)
- 1 Clark
- 1 Junior Clark
- 1 Store Keeper
- 2 Naib Qasid
- 1 Cook
- 1 Nanny
- 1 Security Guard
- 1 Sweeper

ISSUES & SUGGESTIONS:

- Security issues.
  - ➢ There should provide the staff for night to take care for the children.
  - ➢ There is need to resolve the problem of their quarters which are control by wrong authoritative people.

MOTHR & CHILDREN HOME (DARA-UL-FALAH)

Mother & Children Home (Dara-ul-Falah) was situated on Maoza Tarf Mubabrak Awal Nishat Collage Road, Near Lodhi Colony Multan. This institution was eastablished on 16 december 1974. According to PC-1, there were approved 30 families along with their children.

OBJECTIVES

The objectives of this institution are

- To provide the accommodation for widows divorced & destitute.
- To provide vocational training to families& day scholars.
- Free medical facilities & medicines.
- To provide religious & adult education for inmates & day scholars from near community.
- To provide nursery to primary education along with books & other materials.
- Inmates have been rehabilitated after completion of their one year period & follow up, made after rehabilitation.

STAFF

- 1 superintendent
- 1 accountant/ Assistant
- 1 Religious instructor
- 1 Technical Instructor
- 1 Nursery Teacher
- 1 Junior Clerk
- 1 Maid
- 1 Peon
- 2 Watchman
- 1 Sweeper

ELIGIBILITY FOR ADMISSION IN THE INSTITUTION

This institution is eligible for those females who are

- Widows
- Divorced
- Destitute
- Very Poor

CIRCUMSTANCES UNDER WHICH THE WOMEN TAKE ADMISSION

- Due to non source of income.
- Due to non availability of shelter
- Due to non cooperation of their relatives.

ACTUAL POSITION OF INMATES TODAY

Women	=	15
Children	=	35
Total	=	50

BUDGET OF THE YEAR 2013-2014

District	=	5447000/-
Provisional	=	251000/-
		For first 3 months

PROBLEMS & DIFFICULTIES OF THE INSTITUTION

- Family stipend is poor it may increase up to 6000/- rupees per month per family.
- Advertisement of the scheme is not made properly because of fewer budgets.
- After rehabilitation, no source of follow up & non availability of budget.
- Institution's own building may be provided according to PC-1.
- District budget may be released 100% because rent of the office building & others bills are still pending.

SUGGESTIONS

When we give the money for help to others then it means that we are making our nation restless. We should not give them money; we should give them some work & then give them their exchange of their hard work then they feel happiness that they are earning with their own hands & provide their children of their own hands earnings & there is creating self esteem between these females & their children & children also feel happy that they are not dependent on others, their all necessities are fulfilled by their mother & they feel proud at their mothers & the enthusiasm of hard work is creating between these children because children are the future of Pakistan. From using this procedure, we make our future bright because our next nation will have the enthusiasm of hard work & hard work can make the bright future of any country.

THE BE-NAZIR BHUTTO CRISIS CENTRE FOR WOMEN

The Benazir Bhutto Women's Crisis Centers; the first name of this department was Crisis centre for women which provide essential services to victims of abuse and violence and the Punjab government must make sure they do not close down for lack of funding after the devolution of the Ministry for Women's Development. Its name was changed after the death of Benazir for providing the respect of females. This project was starting in January 2007 in Vehari by Tehmina Doltana. In Punjab, there are total 12 crisis centre for women.

OBJECTIVES

These centers provide

- Free socio-psycho counseling
- Free legal help
- Free medical health facilities

STAFF

In Multan, this centre has the staff which is included on 10 persons.

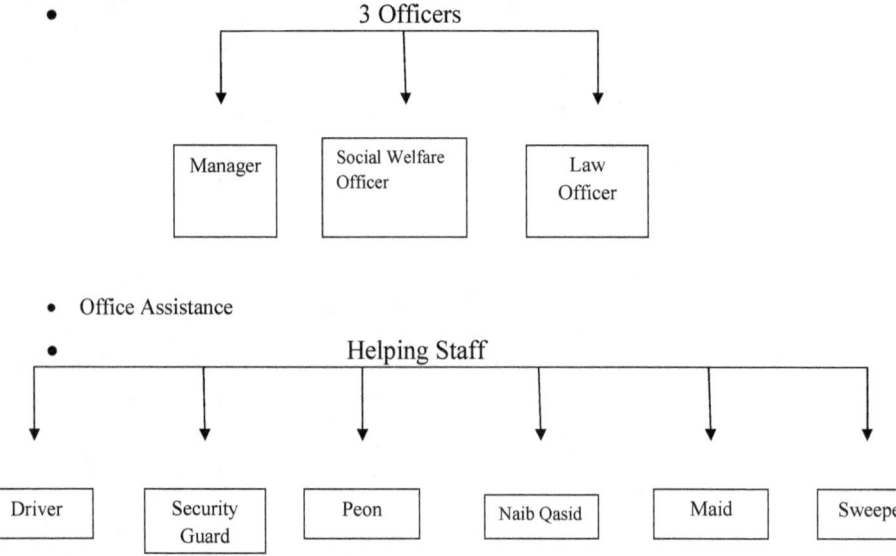

-     3 Officers

| Manager | Social Welfare Officer | Law Officer |

- Office Assistance
-     Helping Staff

| Driver | Security Guard | Peon | Naib Qasid | Maid | Sweeper |

BUDGET: 65 Lacks

ISSUES & SOLUTION

- Increase the authority

  > In our society, mostly people understand the language of stick. So, that's why try to increase their authority & give them 2 police constable 1 male or 1 female. Through increase their authority; they can convict their point easily from people.

DRUG REHABILITATION CENTRE

Drug Rehabilitation Centre was established in Multan at 13 September 2011. This Building is located at Dhear Chowk, Matti Tal Road near Bakhtawar Amin Hospital Multan in front of Gehwara Social Welfare Department. The main purpose of this department is the rehabilitation of addicts who use any type of drugs such as Heroin, Poppy, Hasish, alcoholic & synthetic chemical etc.

OBJECTIVES

There are some objectives of this department are as followed.

- Admission of addicts who use any type of drugs i.e. Heroin, Poppy, Hasish, alcoholic and synthetic   chemical. Detoxification and Treatment of admitted Addicts.
- Preparation of case history of admitted Addicts to analyze their Psychological, Social and Emotional   back   grounds. Counseling and guidance of drug addicts.
- Vocational Training skills and job placement of treated addicts.
- Follow up services to reduce chances of relapse in treated patients.

FACILITIES AVAILBALE FOR PUBLIC

Facilities Which are available for patients are

- Free Treatment
- Free Medicines
- Free Residence (VIP)
- Free Food
- Free Vocational Training
- Job Placement after Rehabilitation (if available)

ISSUES

Mafia Group is become a hurdle in the working of hospital. This group leaves their people in the disguise of patients & they supply drugs & also entice them for using drugs among those patients who are trying to rehabilitate.

SUGGESTION

- For solving the problem of mafia group & for making the better condition of this department: all those previous patients who are taking rehabilitation of this department should be far away from new admitted patients.
- There should be strickly blood test about drugs that from how much times they are using drugs. From blood test, we can stop these people.
- Stop as like people who are working for this group is not enough we should have to stop this group. If you just trap those people who are working for them not say or arrest them so, we can reach the real criminal, govt. should give them strictly punishment even hanged them that they are finishing the future of our country for their personal benefit.

GEHWARA SOCIAL WELFARE DEPARTMENT MULTAN

Children are the future of any country. So, The Punjab government was established a centre for newborn babies, in Multan where children will be nourished till the age of seven, the name of this department was Gehwara.

OBJECTIVES

- To provide protection & care to the 0-7 years children which are abandoned.
- To provide food, shelter, clothing, medical care & school education.
- To provide foster care services to admitted children.
- To make necessary arrangements for those families who are interested for their adaptation.
- Placement of these children after the age of 6 or 7 in other referral institutions such as SOS, Modern Orphanages Centre for their education, rehabilitation & training.
- Follow up to adopted, placed or rehabilitated children at daily basis.

STAFF

- Social Welfare Officer
- Computer Operator
- Nurse
- Assistant/ Accountant
- House Mother
- Junior Clark
- Store Keeper
- Maid
- Cook
- Peon
- Naib Qasid
- Sweeper
- Washer man

SUGGESTION

- There should give the job to as like women that who have no their own children from this step, they can easily understand their grief & not give the preference to their own children but give fully attention & love to these children. From this step, not remains any type of deficiency between them.
- There should be toys for playing these children that they don't feel that they are living in any department.

WELFARE HOME FOR OLD & INFIRM PERSONS (AAFIAT)

Due to industrialization & urbanization, the joint family system is breaking up & the socio-economic structure is disturbed & mostly families don't understand the value of parents. There was need of an institute which provides shelter, food, clothes, health care facilities & recreational facilities to all those people who have no one to look after. Government has established this institute in Multan which is working in industrial estates. Old Age Home was established in 1992 & this department provided services to all those people who are above from 50. The inmates are provided free shelter, food, training treatment rehabilitation, guidance & counseling.

STAFF

- 1 Social Welfare Officer
- 1 Assistenent
- 2 Naib Qasid
- 1Peon
- 1 Sweeper
- 1 Female Attendant
- 1 Washer man
- 1 Driver

SUGGESTION

- This department should firstly try to do the self grooming of the children of those parents who don't want to take care of them. Try to tell them the value of parents. After counseling, if they don't understand then provide them all the facilities.
- There should be a little programs organized between them in which they participate & live happy such like buz-e-adab or any other game which make them active & healthy & also which help them to forget their grief for some time.